Geology Zone

Minerals

by Julie Murray

Dash!
LEVELED READERS
An Imprint of Abdo Zoom • abdobooks.com

Level 1 – Beginning
Short and simple sentences with familiar words or patterns for children who are beginning to understand how letters and sounds go together.

Level 2 – Emerging
Longer words and sentences with more complex language patterns for readers who are practicing common words and letter sounds.

Level 3 – Transitional
More developed language and vocabulary for readers who are becoming more independent.

abdobooks.com

Published by Abdo Zoom, a division of ABDO, PO Box 398166, Minneapolis, Minnesota 55439.

Printed in the United States of America, North Mankato, Minnesota.
102024
012025

Photo Credits: Getty Images, Science Source, Shutterstock
Production Contributors: Kenny Abdo, Jennie Forsberg, Grace Hansen, John Hansen
Design Contributors: Candice Keimig, Neil Klinepier

Library of Congress Control Number: 2024936540

Publisher's Cataloging in Publication Data

Names: Murray, Julie, author.
Title: Minerals / by Julie Murray
Description: Minneapolis, Minnesota : Abdo Zoom, 2025 | Series: Geology zone | Includes online resources and index.
Identifiers: ISBN 9781098287177 (lib. bdg.) | ISBN 9781098287870 (ebook) | ISBN 9781098288228 (Read-to-me ebook)
Subjects: LCSH: Minerals--Juvenile literature. | Hard rock minerals--Juvenile literature. | Rocks--Identification--Juvenile literature. | Geology--Juvenile literature. | Earth sciences--Juvenile literature.
Classification: DDC 549--dc23

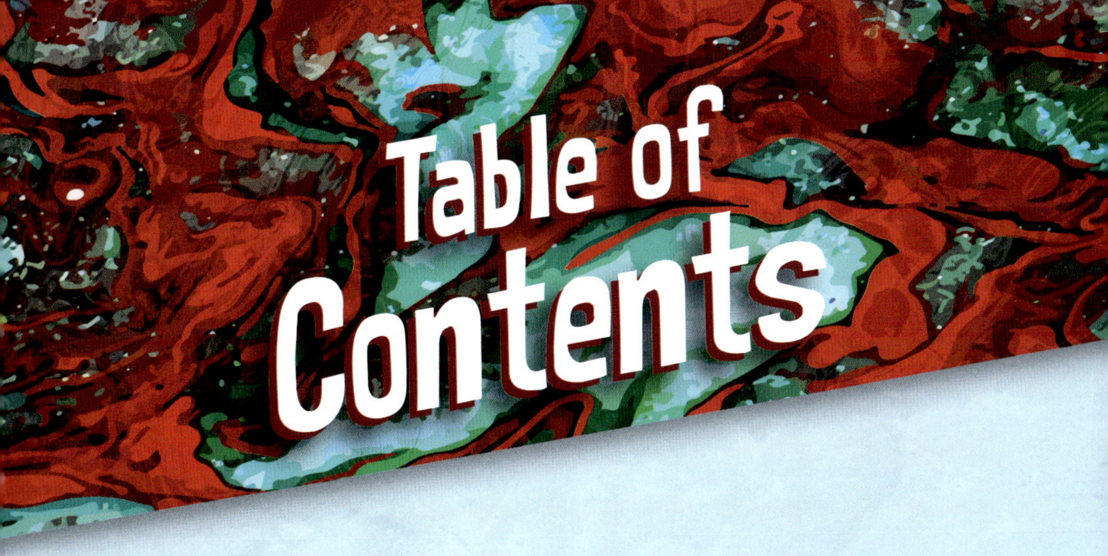
Table of
Contents

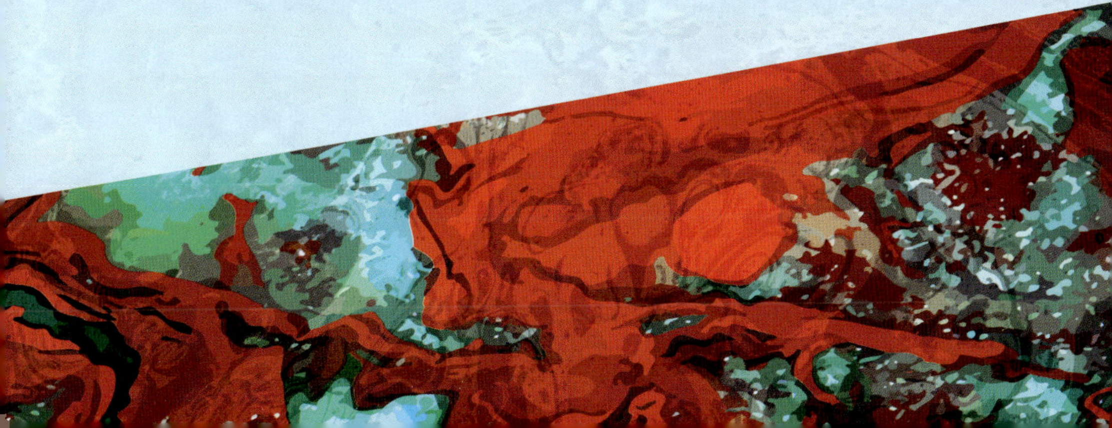

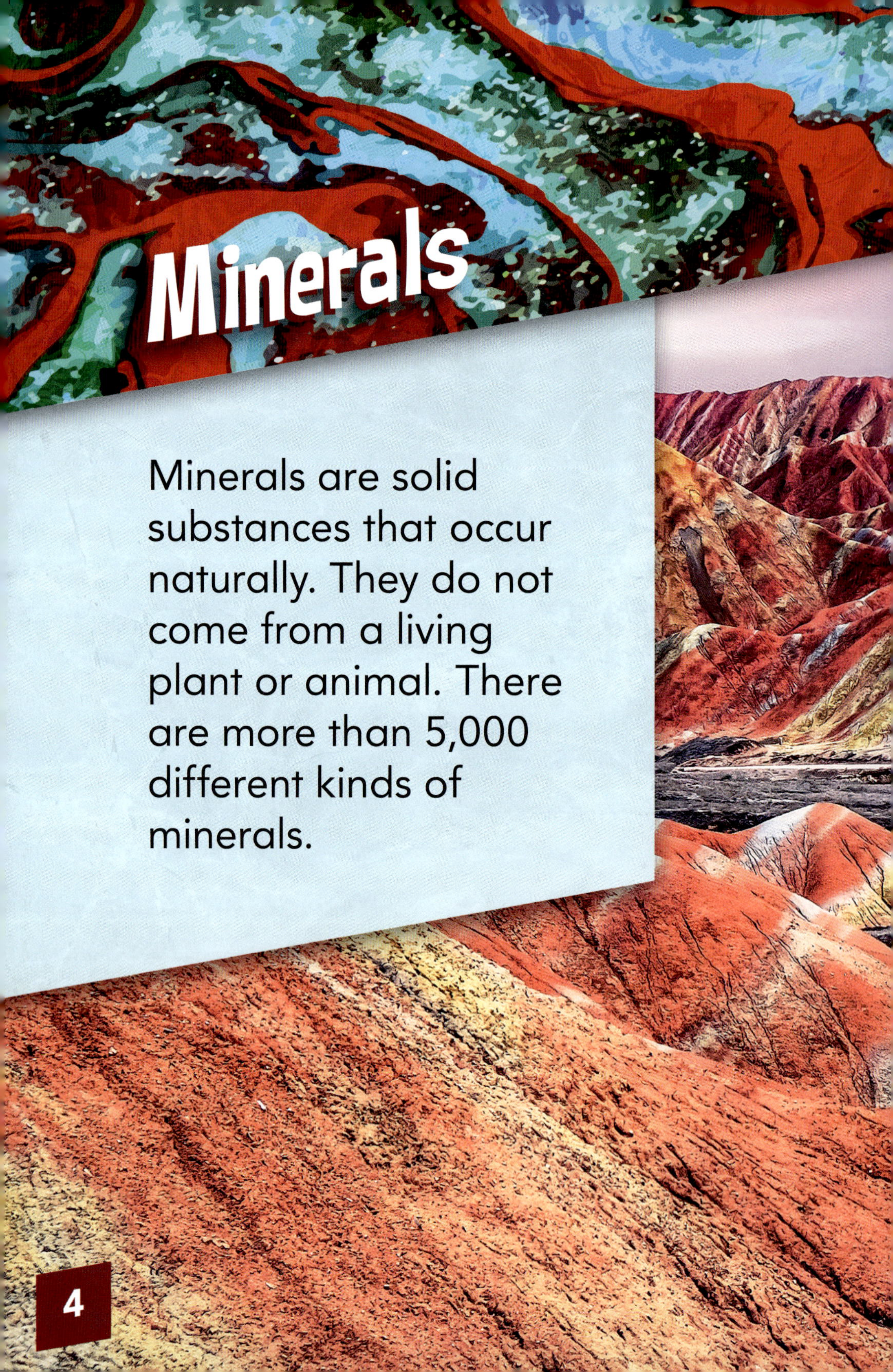

Minerals

Minerals are solid substances that occur naturally. They do not come from a living plant or animal. There are more than 5,000 different kinds of minerals.

6

Minerals make up Earth's rocks, sand, and soils. They are found on the Earth's surface and deep underground. Some rocks are made of only one kind of mineral, such as **limestone**. Others contain many minerals.

Periodic Table of the Elements

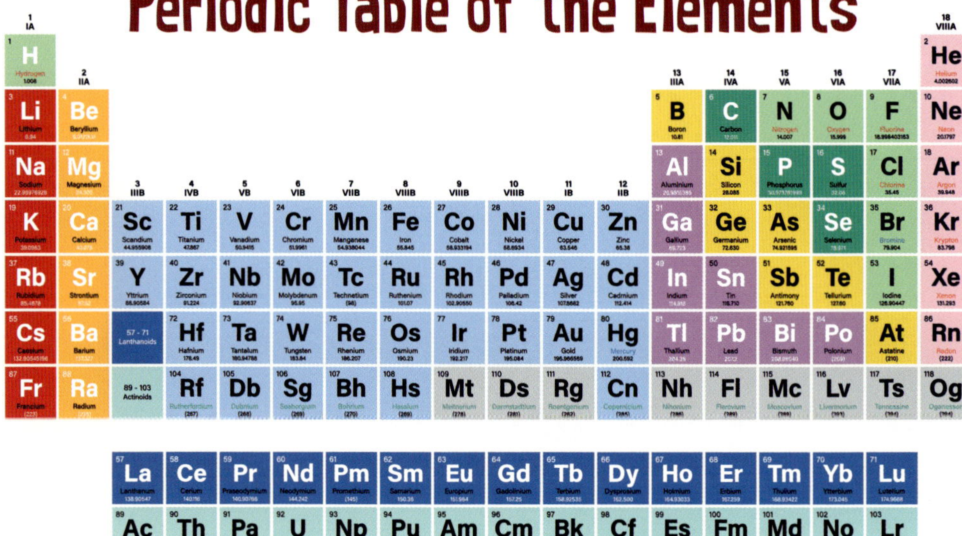

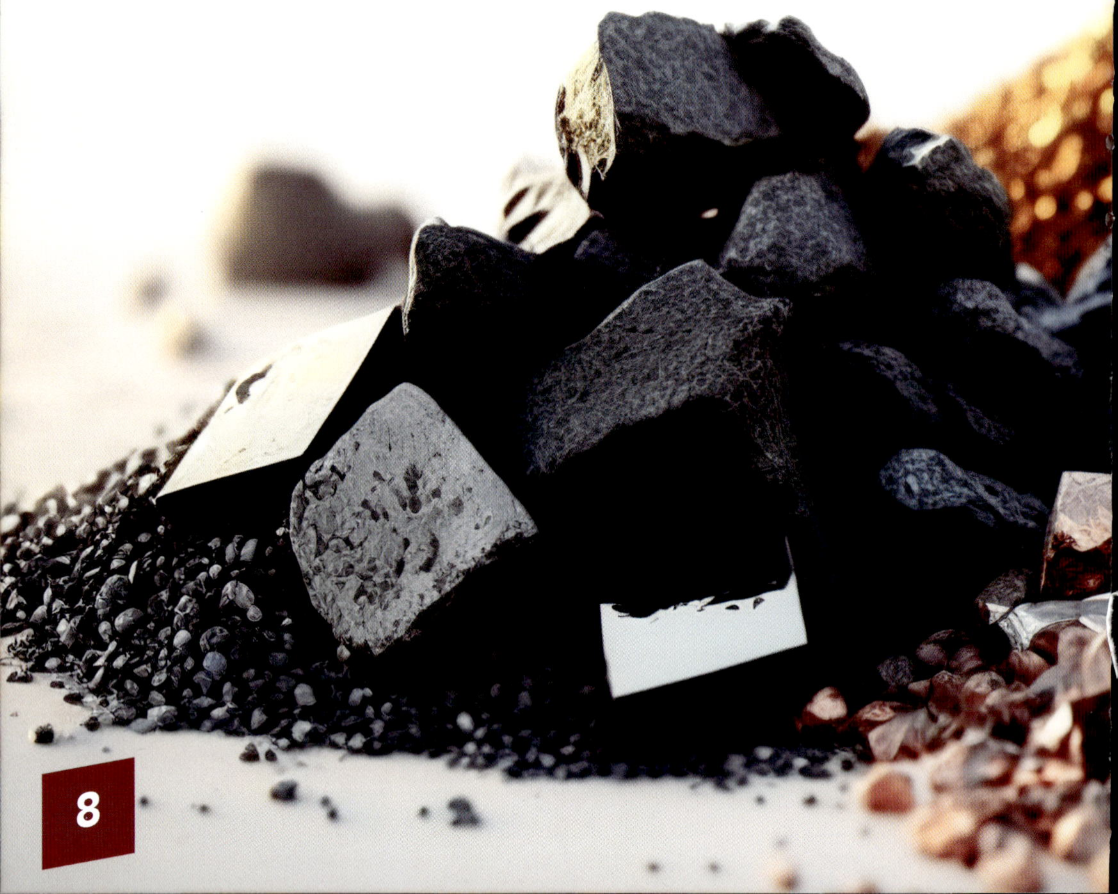

Minerals are made up of elements. Most minerals contain two or more elements. There are 118 different elements. Each element is made from only one type of **atom**.

Crystal Systems

Cubic
Fluorite

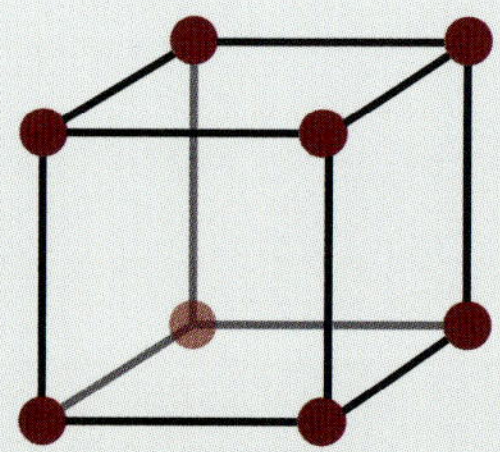

Tetragonal
Wulfenite

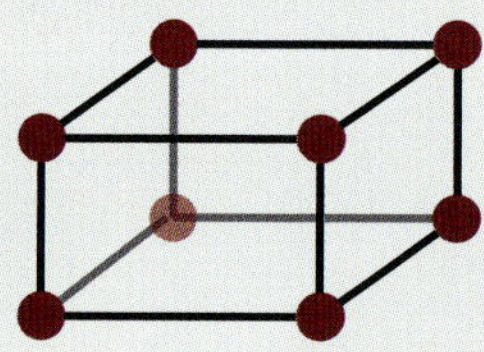

Orthorhombic
Tanzanite

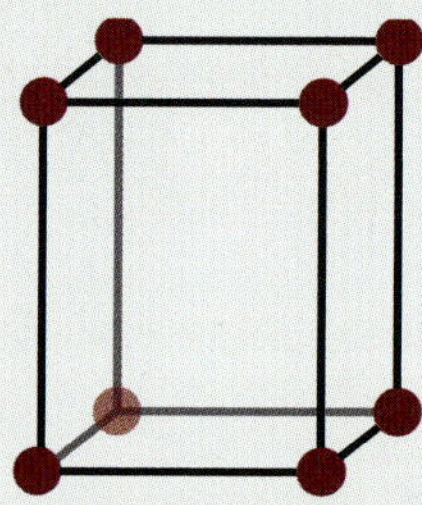

Monoclinic
Arurite

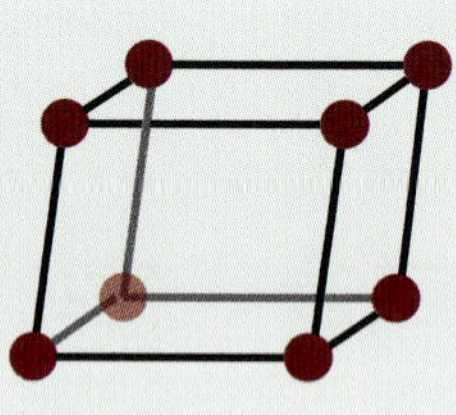

Atoms bond together in a repeating pattern to form a crystal shape. Each crystal has a shape that fits into one of the seven crystal systems.

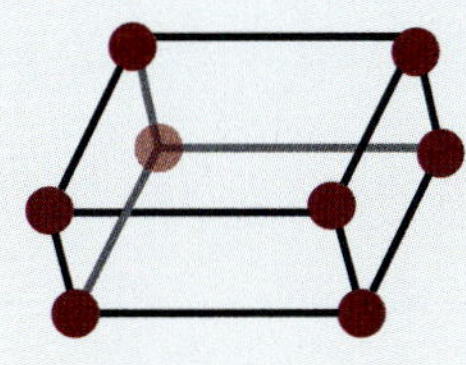

Triclinic

Amazonite

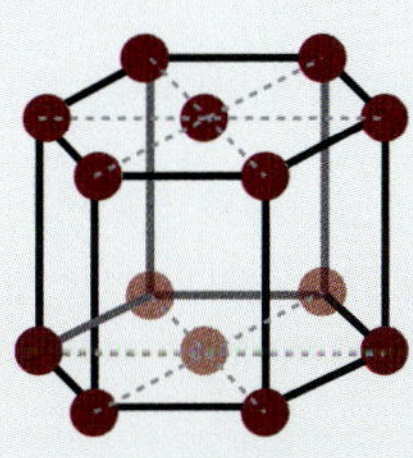

Hexagonal

Emerald

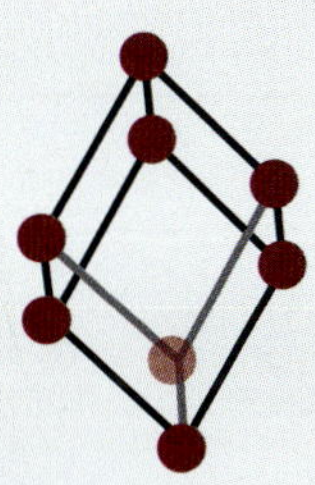

Trigonal

Rhodochrosite

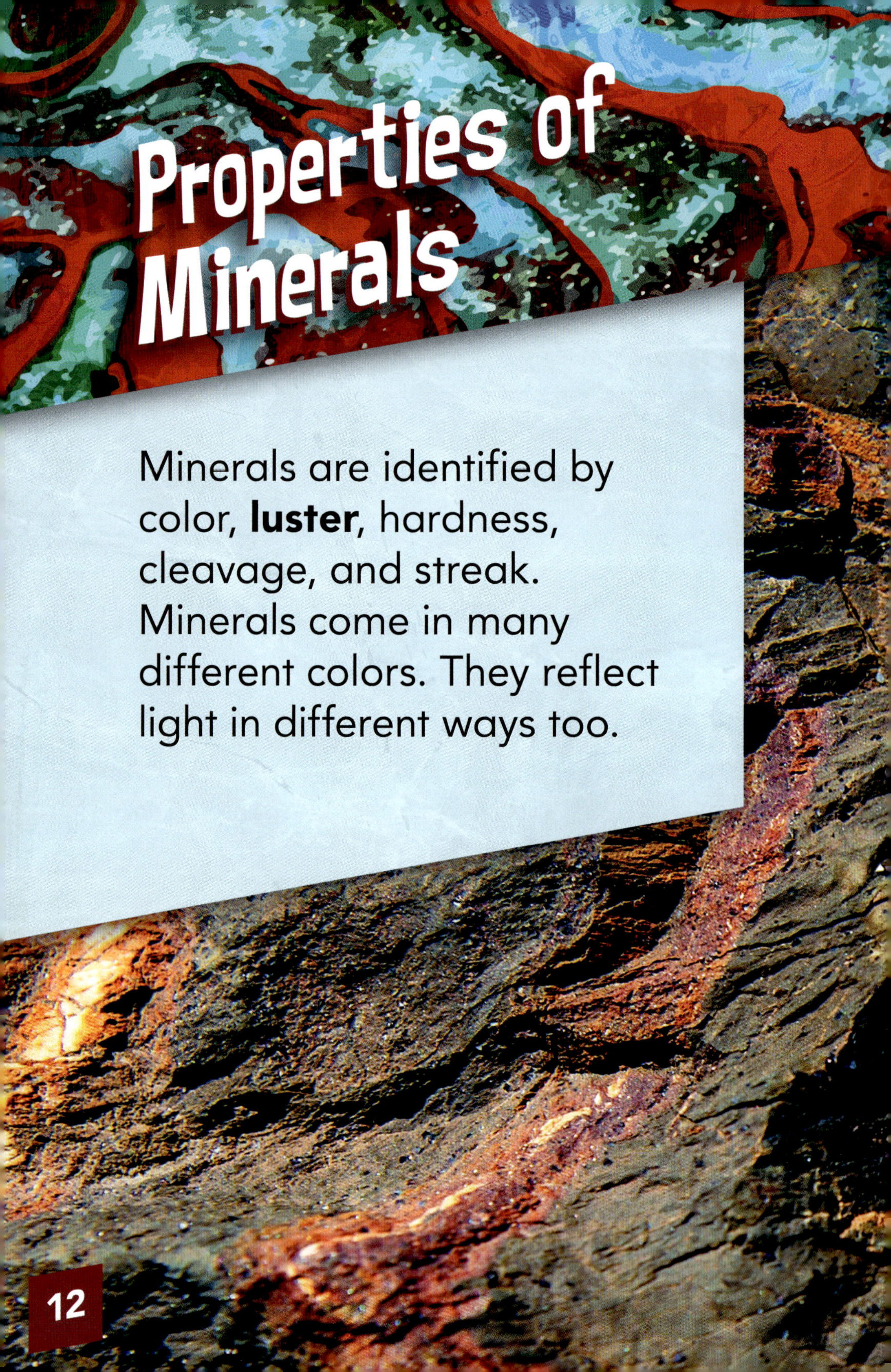

Properties of Minerals

Minerals are identified by color, **luster**, hardness, cleavage, and streak. Minerals come in many different colors. They reflect light in different ways too.

Mohs Hardness Scale

Identifying Minerals

The Mohs Hardness Scale is used to identify minerals by measuring their hardness. The higher the number, the harder the mineral. Diamonds are the hardest mineral.

Mica

Cleavage refers to the way some minerals break. For example, mica breaks in thin, flat sheets. Streak refers to the color of a mineral's powder.

Minerals Around Us

Minerals can be **mined** deep in the Earth. Some of these minerals include gold, silver, and iron.

Minerals are all around us. We use things made from minerals every day. Salt, paint, and toothpaste all have minerals in them. Fluoride is a mineral that is found in toothpaste.

More Facts

- All plants, animals, and humans need minerals to live and grow.
- Minerals made up of one element are called native minerals. Some examples of native minerals are gold, copper, silver, and sulfur.
- Minerals are used in technology, such as televisions, smartphones, and computers.

Glossary

atom – the smallest possible unit of a chemical element.

limestone – a rock formed mostly from shells and other animal remains.

luster – the shine of a surface that softly reflects light.

mined – obtained from a mine.

Index

Online Resources

To learn more about minerals, please visit **abdobooklinks.com** or scan this QR code. These links are routinely monitored and updated to provide the most current information available.